J 297.36 Sch
Schuh, Mari C.
Crayola   Ramadan and Eid
al-Fitr colors

$6.99

W9-AMN-152

1809865

3 4028 10284 6848
HARRIS COUNTY PUBLIC LIBRARY

Crayola

CRAYOLA RAMADAN AND EID AL-FITR COLORS

MARI SCHUH

LERNER PUBLICATIONS ◆ MINNEAPOLIS

FOR NATALIE

Special thanks to content consultant Cawo Abdi, PhD, Department of Sociology, College of Liberal Arts, University of Minnesota

Copyright © 2019 by Lerner Publishing Group, Inc.

All rights reserved. International copyright secured. No part of this book may be reproduced, stored in a retrieval system, or transmitted in any form or by any means—electronic, mechanical, photocopying, recording, or otherwise—without the prior written permission of Lerner Publishing Group, Inc., except for the inclusion of brief quotations in an acknowledged review.

© 2019 Crayola, Easton, PA 18044-0431. Crayola Oval Logo, Crayola, Serpentine Design, Pink Sherbert, and Denim are registered trademarks of Crayola used under license.

Official Licensed Product
Lerner Publications Company
A division of Lerner Publishing Group, Inc.
241 First Avenue North
Minneapolis, MN 55401 USA

For reading levels and more information, look up this title at www.lernerbooks.com.

Main body text set in Billy Infant Regular 24/30.
Typeface provided by SparkyType.

Library of Congress Cataloging-in-Publication Data

Names: Schuh, Mari C., 1975- author.
Title: Crayola ® Ramadan and Eid al-Fitr colors / Mari Schuh.
Description: Minneapolis : Lerner Publications, 2018. | Series: Crayola ® holiday colors | Includes bibliographical references and index.
Identifiers: LCCN 2018006632 (print) | LCCN 2017046671 (ebook) | ISBN 9781541512481 (eb pdf) | ISBN 9781541510937 (lb : alk. paper) | ISBN 9781541527515 (pb : alk. paper)
Subjects: LCSH: Ramadan—Juvenile literature. | Fasts and feasts—Islam—Juvenile literature.
Classification: LCC BP186.4 (print) | LCC BP186.4 .S325 2018 (ebook) | DDC 297.3/6—dc23

LC record available at https://lccn.loc.gov/2018006632

Manufactured in the United States of America
1-43977-33991-2/1/2018

TABLE OF CONTENTS

WHAT IS RAMADAN?

Ramadan has begun. It is a Muslim holy month of prayer and fasting.

Many different colors fill the days and nights of Ramadan.

Let's celebrate!

A crescent moon has a curved shape. It looks like a banana or a boat.

The **BLUE** sky gets darker.

The bright moon shines in the night sky.

Ramadan begins and ends with a crescent moon.

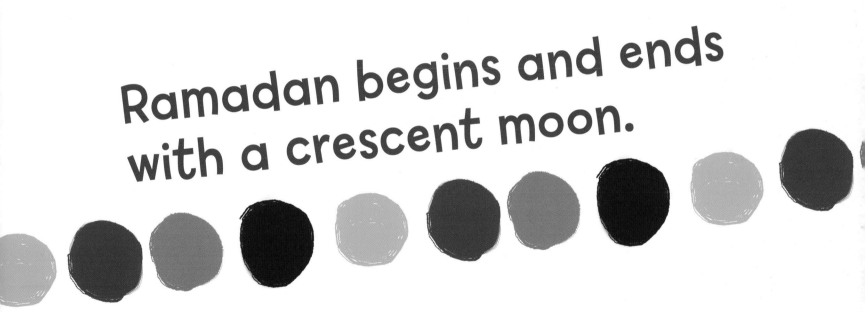

WHAT HAPPENS DURING RAMADAN?

During Ramadan, people do not eat while the sun is in the sky.

When the sun goes down, meals begin with **BROWN** dates and other treats.

During Ramadan, people do not eat or drink between sunrise and sunset.

PURPLE, **RED**, **BLUE**, and **GREEN** colors light up the night.

Bright lights hang in streets and homes during Ramadan.

People use lanterns and lamps during Ramadan.

Colorful designs cover prayer rugs.

People focus on their family, friends, and faith during Ramadan.

CELEBRATING EID AL-FITR

When Ramadan ends, a festival called Eid al-Fitr begins.

It's time to celebrate!

These children celebrate with colorful balloons.

Children play and have fun.
Families and friends enjoy
one another.

People give gifts
and toys.

People buy food to make special meals during Eid al-Fitr.

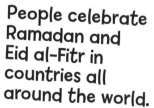

People celebrate Ramadan and Eid al-Fitr in countries all around the world.

They shop for **RED** and **GREEN** vegetables.

Many **ORANGE** and **BROWN** fruits are used for meals too.

People eat sweet treats and desserts.

They celebrate the end of the long days of fasting.

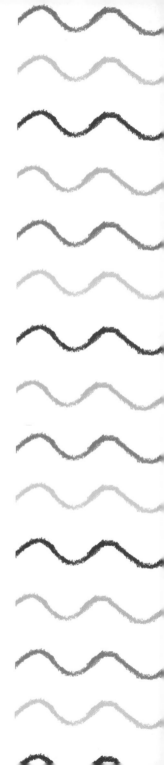

Yellow and red goodies are a sweet way to celebrate.

These women and children wear orange, white, and turquoise to celebrate Eid al-Fitr.

People wear their best clothes during Eid al-Fitr.

Some people buy **COLORFUL** new clothes.

Eid al-Fitr is a time for joy.

People give gifts and money to family members and to those in need.

A golden ribbon makes an Eid al-Fitr gift extra special!

A COLORFUL CELEBRATION

Color is all around during Ramadan and Eid al-Fitr.

These colorful days are a time to be thankful.

COPY AND COLOR!

Ramadan and Eid al-Fitr are colorful holidays! Here are some of the Crayola® crayon colors used in this book. What colors will you use to celebrate? Copy these pages, and color the symbols of Ramadan and Eid al-Fitr.

PINK SHERBERT

AQUAMARINE

ROYAL PURPLE

GOLDENROD

DENIM

GLOSSARY

celebrate: to do something special to mark a happy occasion

dates: the brown fruit of a palm plant

fasting: a time of no eating or drinking

festival: a time of celebration in honor of a special occasion

holy: having to do with religion or a higher being

Muslim: a person whose religion is Islam

prayer rugs: small rugs people kneel on when praying

TO LEARN MORE

BOOKS

Bailey, R. J. *Ramadan*. Minneapolis: Bullfrog, 2017. Learn about the ways people celebrate Ramadan.

Grack, Rachel. *Ramadan*. Minneapolis: Bellwether Media, 2017. Explore the history of Ramadan and why it is an important holiday.

Sebra, Richard. *It's Ramadan and Eid al-Fitr!* Minneapolis: Lerner Publications, 2017. Read more about the celebrations of Ramadan and Eid al-Fitr.

WEBSITES

Celebrating Ramadan
http://kids.nationalgeographic.com/explore/history/ramadan/
Read about Ramadan and how people celebrate this important holiday.

Ramadan Thoughts
http://www.crayola.com/free-coloring-pages/print/ramadan-thoughts-coloring-page/
Color a Ramadan design, and then add your thoughts for the next year.

Star and Crescent Moon Mobile
https://www.activityvillage.co.uk/star-and-crescent-moon-mobile
Learn how to make a star and crescent moon mobile with only a few supplies.

Harris County Public Library
Houston, Texas

INDEX

PHOTO ACKNOWLEDGMENTS

The images in this book are used with the permission of: James Strachan/Getty Images, p. 1; Lawkeeper/Shutterstock.com, pp. 2, 30, 31, 32, 33 (geometric design); arapix/Shutterstock.com, p. 4; Zephyr_p/Shutterstock.com, p. 5 (top left); JOAT/Shutterstock.com, pp. 5 (top right), 21, 25; nobtis/iStock /Getty Images, p. 5 (bottom left); MidoSemsem/Shutterstock.com, p. 5 (bottom right); Allexxandar/Shutterstock.com, p. 6; photosimysia/Shutterstock.com, p. 9; LanaDjuric/Getty Images, p. 10; LiliGraphie/Shutterstock.com, p. 11; Thierry Bresillon/Corbis Documentary/Getty Images, pp. 12-13; Yawar Nazir/Getty Images, p. 15; Sabir Mazhar/Anadolu Agency/Getty Images, pp. 16-17; Md.Saiful Aziz Shamseer/Wikimedia Commons (CC 1.0 PDM), p. 18; gvictoria/Shutterstock.com, p. 19; Distinctive Images/Shutterstock.com, p. 22; Chumsak Kanoknan/Getty Images, p. 26; Mila Supinskaya GlashchenkoShutterstock.com, p. 27; © Laura Westlund/Independent Picture Service, pp. 28, 29 (illustrations).

Cover: JOAT/Shutterstock.com (gifts); James Strachan/Stone/Getty Images (mosque); AHMAD GHARABLI/AFP/Getty Images (crescent moon).